THE ULTIMATE BOOK OF
Quilt
Labels

Margo J. Clabo

That Patchwork Place®

An Imprint of
Martingale & Company

Credits

Editor-in-Chief	Kerry I. Smith
Technical Editor	Janet White
Managing Editor	Judy Petry
Design Director	Cheryl Stevenson
Cover Designer	Trina Stahl
Text Designer	Cheryl Stevenson
Design Assistant	Marijane E. Figg
Copy Editor	Liz McGehee
Illustrator	Robin Strobel
Photographer	Brent Kane

The Ultimate Book of Quilt Labels
© 1998 by Margo J. Clabo
Martingale & Company, PO Box 118,
Bothell, WA 98041-0118 USA

Printed in the United States of America
03 02 01 00 99 98 6 5 4 3 2 1

Library of Congress Cataloging-in-Publication Data

Clabo, Margo,
    The ultimate book of quilt labels / Margo Clabo.
       p.   cm. — (The joy of quilting)
    ISBN 1-56477-146-6
    1. Quilts—Labeling—Design. 2. Labels—Design I. Title.
II. Series.
TT835.C55   1998
746.46—dc21
                               97-48429
                                  CIP

Dedication

In loving memory of Mother, Mary Eugenia Bivins Jenkins, who taught me how to match plaids and encouraged in me the attitude that I could do anything if I was willing to try; and Daddy, Jim Mitchell Jenkins, who taught me the value of recycling and the knack of packing a lot of stuff into a little bit of space; to Genevieve and Fred Clabo, for their unconditional love and support; and most especially to Alvin, Jason, and Joshua—my love and my joy.

Acknowledgments

This project would not have been possible without the contributions of many friends, both longtime and newly found. Quilting friends truly are "sew special." Thank you all from the bottom of my heart, for sharing your work and for meeting my deadlines!

Mission Statement

We are dedicated to providing quality products and service by working together to inspire creativity and to enrich the lives we touch.

Table of Contents

Introduction

I must confess that I did not make labels for my own quilts until recently. One day, I unpacked a fairly new quilt and could not remember when I had made it. Early 1990s seemed a vague date for such a recently completed quilt. I realized that I needed labels for my own reference as well as for the possibility that some of my quilts might someday be considered treasured heirlooms (even if they are not masterpieces). Most of my quilts are made to be used up and loved to death, but if any do survive my family's affections, I would like them to carry a label with information that a future quilt owner might find interesting.

Like most quilt lovers, I own several old quilts that I have either inherited or purchased. None of them has a label to tell who made them, when, or why. The quilts that we believe were made by my husband's grandmother have no labels. How wonderful it would be to know for sure that she did make these quilts and when. The quilt my grandmother supposedly made, using fabric she cut from garments that were never retrieved from the dry-cleaning shop where she worked, carries no documentation to support that family legend.

Many current quilting books contain instructions for creating great, new quilts. Somewhere near the end of the book there is usually a paragraph or two about the importance of documenting your quilt and maybe some brief instructions on how to make a label. I tried making some, but my handwritten labels were disappointing, and I do not enjoy embroidery, so I started searching for alternative techniques. Ready-made fabric labels, which are quick and easy, did not always complement or coordinate with my quilts. I experimented with an old typewriter, then progressed to the computer. The more I explored, the more possibilities I found for printing graphics and text onto fabric to make unique, informative labels.

This book contains some of the techniques and ideas I have used for making custom labels. You will learn how to make several types of labels, beginning with traditional methods and working up to computer-generated text and graphics. You do not need any fancy equipment to make great labels, but a computer or high-tech sewing maching provides more options.

I encourage you to use the information here to create original labels that will truly be the final stitch in your quilt. Every quilt deserves to be documented. If it is an antique, include all of the known information, including when and where you got it. Even if you don't know who made it, let the documentation begin with today's information. If it is a new quilt, who, what, when, where, and why are just the beginning.

The first section of this book provides general information about labels, including what to write and where to attach it. The second section explains the different techniques used to make labels, from simple inking on fabric to scanning images with a computer. The color gallery features twenty-three quilts and their labels, made with a variety of techniques explained in the book. Three copy-art designs are provided, and you are welcome to trace them for your own *personal* use. These copyrighted designs may not be reproduced for any other purpose without the designer's permission. An extensive list of mail-order sources is included for your use if you cannot find products in your local quilt shop or fabric stores, along with numerous Web sites and e-mail addresses where you can find more information.

Mention of a particular brand-name item in this book does not mean it is the only or best product or service for a particular application, only that it was tried. Product testing is always recommended for your projects. If you try any of the products mentioned in the book, let the folks know that you heard about it here!

General Information

The Importance of Documentation

Until the early 1800s, quilts were simply considered necessary household items rather than a legacy to be passed down, so few carry the names of their makers. Making quilts was just another household chore, and women seldom thought of signing their names to their quilts. Often, a quilt was the most beautiful thing a family owned, and the quilter deserved to be recognized for creating it, but it is a rare treat for us to find a label signifying the maker's pride of workmanship. Because I am not a quilt historian, I went to several quilting friends who know more about these things than I do for information about labels on old quilts and the importance of documenting today's quilts.

Bets Ramsey, artist and quilt historian, has this to say about labels:

When the last stitch is put into a quilt and the edge is finished, its maker can rejoice in the completion of a challenging task. She will always be able to enjoy pride in her workmanship and the gratification of successful accomplishment, even if she never wins a blue ribbon for her efforts. But wait, one final thing must be added before the quilt is ready for display and admiration. It needs a signature, a date, and other information to perpetuate its history long after the quilter's voice is hushed.

The quilts made today will become the family heirlooms of tomorrow, just as our mothers' and grandmothers' quilts became our own treasures. Family members and quilt historians will want to know the histories of the quilts this generation has made, and there is no better time to record that important information than the moment when the binding is finished. A label assures the maker that her quilt's story will be preserved.

Merikay Waldvogel, author, quilt historian, and active member of the American Quilt Study Group, says:

Finding inscriptions either appliquéd, embroidered, or inked is an exciting discovery for anyone examining an old quilt, because the information provides clues to the history of unattributed quilts [anonymous quiltmakers]. Most inscriptions appear on the quilt top and were applied as the quilt was constructed. Sarah Berry, a Tennessee quiltmaker working in the late 1800s, boldly appliquéd her initials, a year, and sometimes a quilt's name on her quilts. According to family stories, Sarah Berry made a quilt for each of her twenty-five grandchildren before she died in 1898. Since then, those quilts were dispersed throughout the United States. Because she labeled her quilts, quilt historians one hundred years later were able to locate thirteen Sarah Berry quilts as the family genealogy was compiled.

There is another important reason for labeling your quilts. Documentation is the key for proving the ownership of a lost or stolen quilt. Obtaining documentation by a certified appraiser describing the quilt and its known history, whether an old quilt or a new one, is the best way to ensure that an insurance company will pay a claim for a lost or stolen quilt. Without a certified appraisal, you will only be reimbursed for what it would take to purchase bedding from a department store, not the actual worth of your handmade treasure. Although a label is not necessary for an insurance claim to be paid, it is useful for the appraisal and for tracing a missing quilt. Keep photographs of the quilt and the label with the written appraisal in a safe place. If a quilt is stolen, the label will probably be removed unless it is an integral part of the quilt; but if a quilt is lost, the information on the label may be what brings it back to you!

Laura Chapman, who teaches a label-making class at Jinny Beyer's annual Hilton Head Seminar, shared this story with me:

I remember so well the moment that I discovered a quiltmaker's initials and a date intricately appliquéd into the border of an antique quilt that I had just purchased. It made my heart jump to see her initials 'P.F.K.,' and I felt an immediate connection to her. I began to wonder about her life in 1932. Where did she live? What prompted her to undertake the complex appliqué, and how did she learn to make such tiny stitches? I also began to realize that she was awfully proud of her original design, and felt sufficiently pleased with the end-product to sign and date her work of art. I wanted to thank her for sharing that little bit of information about herself with me, and let her know that I love her quilt and will be a good caretaker of it. That quilt quickly became one of my favorites.

I have been very fortunate to inherit several quilts that my grandmother and great-grandmother made. Even though I know who made them and that they were made in Texas, I would love to have additional information abut the quilts and their makers. As a bridge between the generations, I believe that we owe it to our daughters and granddaughters to provide them with details about the quilts that we are making today, so that they won't have to wonder about us.

See Laura's quilt on page 29 in the color gallery.

What to Write on Your Quilt Label

Documentation on a quilt can be as scant as initials and a date discreetly quilted into the background, or as extensive as a full history. Some of the techniques described in this book make labeling so easy that you will want to put more detailed information on all of your quilts. At the very least, record who made the quilt, the year it was completed, and the city where it was made. Remember that documentation increases the value of your quilt, historically as well as sentimentally. Keep in mind that some of the information we, as quilt-makers, take for granted is beyond the knowledge of the general public. For that reason, you may even consider including on your quilt's label the amount of time involved in its creation, or the dates it was begun and completed.

In labeling your own quilts, use your full name. Include your nickname, too, if you like. If the quilt is one that you entered into shows, list the shows it appeared in, the dates, the cities, and any awards it received. Or, you may want to make separate labels for each award that the quilt receives.

Award labels for "Quilting Friends are Sew Special"

Remember that the label does not have to be just a listing of the facts either. A sentimental message, chosen especially for the receiver, or original poetry on the label makes the quilt an extra-special gift. Greeting cards are always a good source of thoughtful messages if you have trouble coming up with something original.

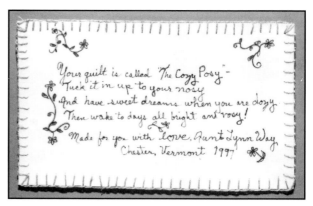

Lynne Way of Chester, Vermont, created this label for her niece by stabilizing fabric with freezer paper and inking her prose and decorative flowers onto it.

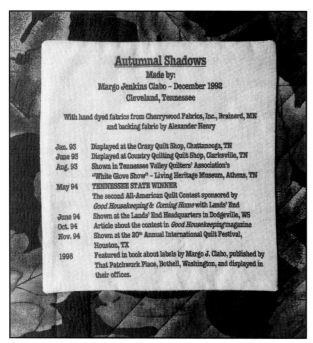

Award label for "Autumnal Shadows"

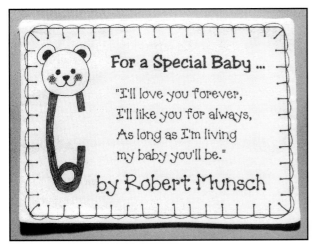

The poem on this computer-generated label is reprinted with permission from the children's book Love You Forever *by Robert Munsch. This label design, including the buttonhole stitch around the edge, is from QuiltClips by Carolyn Kissel, and the font is DJ Doodlers by Dianne Hook of D. J. Inkers.*

"It's Your Quilt," *another wonderful poem for a child's quilt, was written by Nancy Riddell. It was originally published in* Fast Patch Kid's Quilts *by Krause Publications.*

Consider using a graphic that is suggestive of an interesting name.

I used a computer to create this label for Mary Ray Coble's quilt. The sun motif came from a ClickArt Express disk called "Borders, Framers and Bursts."

You might even want to create a quilt label that spells out the laundering instructions, especially if it is for someone who might not know how to care for it properly. Because I have made only one quilt so far with a wool batting, I made this laundry label to remind *myself* of the special washing instructions.

Christmas Rose laundry label by Margo Clabo

If you have an antique quilt in your family with a special story, create a label to tell it and attach it to the quilt so the history will not be lost. The following information was taken from a placard next to an antique quilt at a show several years ago at the Living Heritage Museum in Athens, Tennessee.

This quilt was stolen from a farmyard clothesline, slit in the center with a bayonet, and worn by an unknown Confederate soldier during the final, bitter winter of the Civil War. Short of money and struggling to make his way home to his family after the war, the soldier sold the quilt to future Justice of the Peace John Robert Nelson of Kimberlin Heights (just south of Knoxville, Tennessee). Nelson was himself a Confederate veteran, and he presented the quilt to his wife, Martha Finger Nelson, who repaired the hole that had once accommodated the soldier's head. Flowers were moved from two corner sections to mend the rip in the pattern, but no extra yellow material was available to repair the center stripe. The quilt was used by the Nelson family for many years and passed on to Nelson's daughter, Maude Nelson Johnson, then to her daughter, Ella Ree Johnson Bounds, and is currently in the possession of Nelson's great-grandson, Larry Bounds of Knoxville, Tennessee.

This information was not permanently attached to the quilt, but it would be wise to do so. Without a label, this quilt's fascinating history could become separated from it someday. You never know how long a quilt will last, and you may not always be around to tell its story. A future owner may not remember it accurately.

Always make an effort when you purchase or inherit a quilt to find out everything you can about it, then make a label so the quilt carries its own story. Record all of the information that you know is factual, as well as any oral history of the quilt. If you own an antique quilt but do not know its history, create a label with whatever facts you do know. Let its history begin with today. Tell when, where, and how you came to own it, and leave room for additional information should it become available, or create another label with newfound facts. I really do wish that I knew the story of the 1880s LeMoyne Star quilt I purchased in Houston. I designed this label (shown below) so its story can begin with me.

If there's a special story that relates to a quilt *you've* made, create a label that tells it and attach it to the quilt so the story will not be lost.

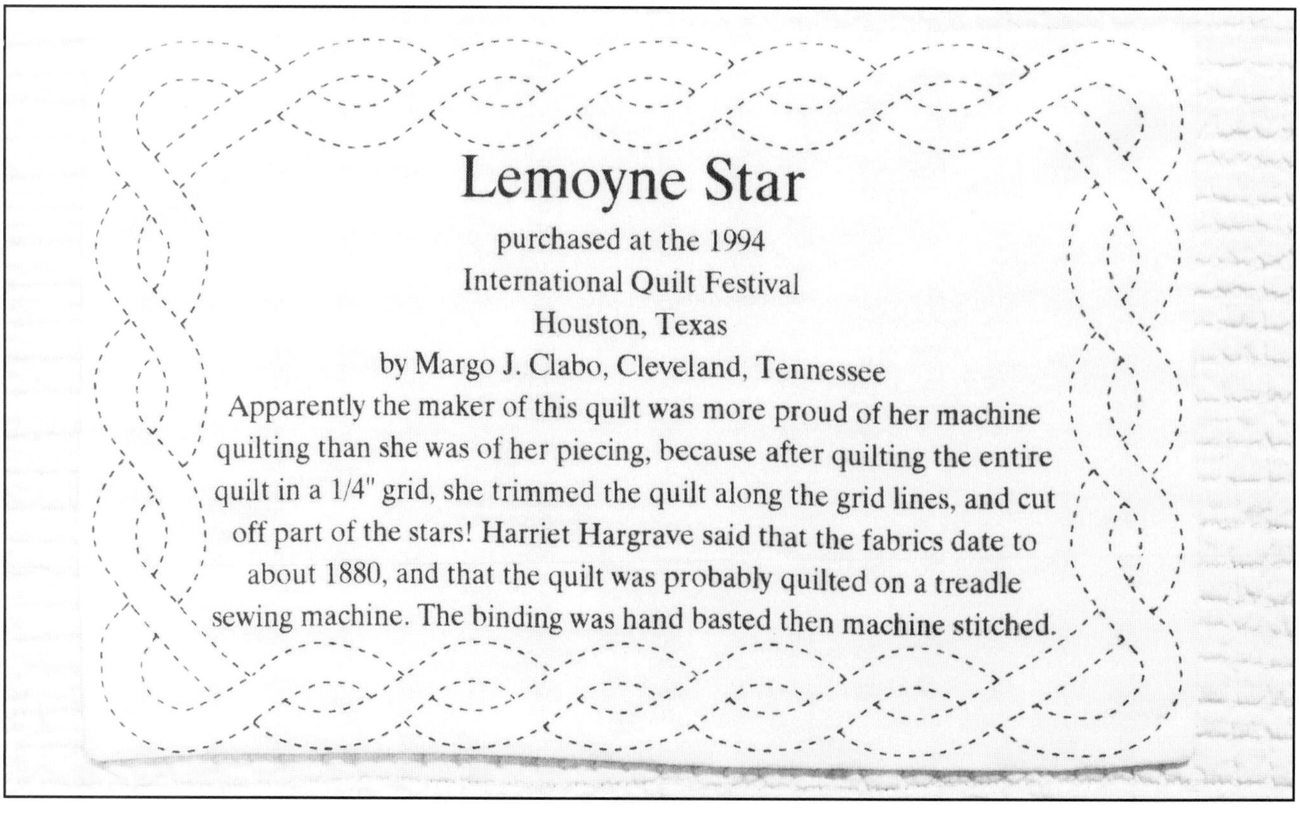

Lemoyne Star

purchased at the 1994
International Quilt Festival
Houston, Texas
by Margo J. Clabo, Cleveland, Tennessee
Apparently the maker of this quilt was more proud of her machine quilting than she was of her piecing, because after quilting the entire quilt in a 1/4" grid, she trimmed the quilt along the grid lines, and cut off part of the stars! Harriet Hargrave said that the fabrics date to about 1880, and that the quilt was probably quilted on a treadle sewing machine. The binding was hand basted then machine stitched.

Use a label to ensure that a quilt's exotic name is remembered. "Dionaea" (page 32) is Latin for "Venus's-flytrap"; "Les Pommes" (page 32) is French for "the apples"; and "Somar Solverv" (page 36) is Norwegian for "summer solstice." Relating the label to the name of the quilt can provide an opportunity for creativity. Some quilt names are humorous. The label can be just as whimsical and fun. The name of Shelby Morris's "Pink Lemonade" quilt (page 29) not only described the colors of the quilt, but made it easy to create a great label!

The type of information you include on the label may depend on the use that will be made of the quilt. A label on a quilt destined for quilt-show competition will not be as sentimental or as decorative as one made for a wedding gift. A baby quilt that will be laundered often will not have the same kind of label as a wall hanging that will never be washed. Use your own judgment about what you want to include on each label you make and the best method for creating it.

Judy Chaney memorialized the inspiration for her quilt and the class where she started it. She printed the text using her computer and added the sewing machine with a rubber stamp.

Barbara Baume's label documented the making of her quilt with four other quilters she met through the Internet. Using a Pigma pen and a banner pattern from Susan McKelvey's Scrolls and Banners to Trace, *she embellished each with different flowers of her own design. Then, she pieced them into blocks to surround the hand-printed story of the quilt.*

Where and How to Attach Your Label

Labels are not usually attached to the front of the quilt, but documentation and identification can be pieced, appliquéd, embroidered, or even quilted into the quilt top.

This label was written freehand directly on the backing with a black Pigma pen. Maude's quilt represents three generations of Clabos.

Initials are worked into the quilting. This sample was made using Hari Walner's techniques from Trapunto by Machine.

Album quilts, friendship quilts, and fund-raising quilts have often been labeled using these methods. On older quilts, the front of the quilt is where you will sometimes find a date, the initials, or even the full name of the quiltmaker. Look for information that is discreetly quilted in, or perhaps pieced or appliquéd into the design of the quilt top.

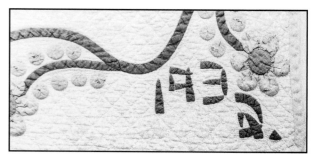

Initials and date on Laura Chapman's antique quilt

It is probably better to create a label and attach it to the back of the quilt. To attach a label in the most permanent way possible, piece it into the backing fabric or appliqué it to the backing fabric and remove the fabric behind the label before quilting. This will make it very difficult to remove the label.

Reverse appliqué can be worked into the backing fabric. This photograph shows only a sample label. A label reverse-appliquéd to the backing of a quilt before quilting would be impossible to remove without leaving a large hole as evidence of tampering.

Probably the most common method of attaching a label is to appliqué it to the back of the quilt after the binding has been completed. Appliqué can be quick and easy, or difficult and time-consuming; the choice is yours.

The easiest, if not the most permanent, way to affix a label is to hand write, type, or use a computer to print text onto fabric, apply a fusible-web backing, and iron it to the back of your quilt. This method is not the one you would use if you were labeling a future heirloom, but it is certainly an option to consider for a wall hanging that will not be laundered or handled much.

Another way to label wall hangings is to write with permanent ink directly on the sleeve fabric. This works especially well if the sleeve fabric is a light color; if the sleeve is dark, you may want to fuse a light-colored label onto it.

You may need to label a quilt for a show with specific information required by the show promoters. If they want the information to be on the quilt,

but covered from the eyes of the judges, you can make a lined label guard and pin it securely over the information on the label. It can easily be re-pinned by the show coordinators to expose the label for interested show visitors! (See page 15 for instructions on making a label guard.)

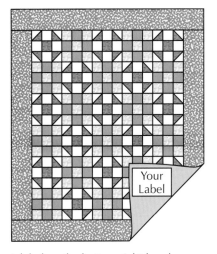

A label on the bottom right-hand corner is easy to display at a quilt show.

If you create a quilted garment, especially a coat or jacket, make a label and appliqué it to the inside of the jacket back, below the back of the collar, or to the inside front like a patch pocket and leave the top unattached. Then you will have a handy place to tuck your "mad money" and shopping list for your next trip to the quilt shop!

There are no hard-and-fast rules about where and how to attach your labels. The important thing is to just do it!

How to Add a Lining

After printing and coloring your label, no matter which method you use, complete it by adding a lining. This not only makes the label more attractive because there is no shadowing of light fabric around the edges, but it also makes a finished edge that is easy to appliqué around.

In the sample above, the edges of the fabric in the top label show through the light label. No edges show through the lined label on the bottom.

1. Use spray starch to stabilize the lining fabric, then place the lining fabric right sides together with the completed label and either press so the two fabrics stick together by static or carefully pin so they won't shift.
2. If the shape has straight edges, trim it ⅜" from the completed label design to allow a ⅛" border around it.

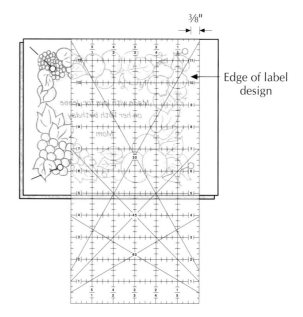

3. With the unstarched label fabric on the bottom so the feed dogs will ease it along without stretching it, stitch completely around the label edges, using a ¼" seam and beginning at the middle of one of the sides. Pivot at each corner with your needle in the down position and end by stitching over the beginning stitches.
4. Press the label to set the seams and trim the corners, being very careful not to cut the stitching.

5. Pinch and pull the two layers apart so you can safely cut a small slit in the center of the lining fabric without clipping the front of the label. Turn the label right side out through the slit and use a point turner to gently shape the corners. If the label does not have angled corners, smooth all of the turned edges from the inside.

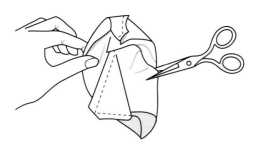

6. Press the completed label unit and cover the slit with a "Band-Aid" made of lining fabric and fusible web if desired.

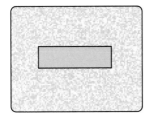

7. Hand appliqué the finished unit to the back of your quilt, using a blind hem stitch. Catch just the lining fabric and the quilt backing with your needle, and your label will appear to float on the surface of the quilt back with no visible means of attachment.

If you like the look of a "floating" label but don't like to do handwork, replace the lining fabric with a fusible interfacing and simply fuse the completed label unit to the back of the quilt. However, if you use this method, be sure to skip all of the ironing in the previous instructions.

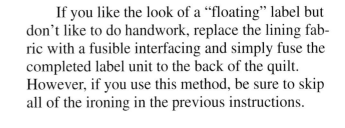

Label Guards

You can make a special label guard to cover the label information from the eyes of a quilt-show judge. One of the major complaints that I hear from judges and show coordinators about labels is that the label either is not covered securely and the judge inadvertently sees the maker's name, or the cover is stitched so securely that is difficult to remove for the show.

Use the lining instructions above to create a separate guard piece that can be pinned over your label. However, instead of slitting the lining and adding a "Band-Aid," leave an opening on one side seam and slipstitch it closed after turning the piece right side out. The label guard can easily be removed by the show coordinators to expose the informative and decorative label for interested show visitors.

Techniques

Ready-made Labels

If you are in a hurry and don't want to take the time to design your own label, ready-made options are available at your local quilt shop or fabric store. Several fabrics sold by the yard have labels of different styles and sizes printed on them. They are ready for you to cut apart, fill in the desired information, and attach to your quilt.

Fusible web can be used to stabilize fabric so writing on it is easier. Then you can simply fuse the label to the quilt, and you will be finished in a jiffy. Or, you can stabilize the label by taping it to your tabletop or pressing it onto a piece of freezer paper. After you complete the text, just remove the paper and appliqué the label to the back of your quilt. Remember to follow the manufacturer's instructions if heat setting is necessary to make your text more permanent. This preprinted option is nice if the style is something you like, and the size and colors are right for your project.

Labels by the yard are available in quilt and fabric shops. These yardage samples were designed by Susan McKelvey, Magaret & Slusser, and Debbi Mumm. The preprinted label for Christmas Rose is a Magaret & Slusser design from Watercolor Impressions *by SST. Blest be the Tie was inked by hand on a preprinted label by Susan McKelvey.*

Labor of Love and other Signature labels from Block Party Studios and Fancywork labels by Kathy O'Hara Light. Kathy's nostalgic labels are silk-screened in golden brown on premium 100% cotton muslin and blend with brown Pigma pens; the "Victorian" labels are a soft black and blend with black Pigmas. All of the labels may be hand colored with permanent fabric pens for a delightful, personalized antique look.

A good friend of mine, Lynne Demeter of Cleveland, Tennessee, surprised me with a wonderful miniature Flying Geese quilt that she paper-pieced using scraps in warm country colors. Lynne used a brown Pigma pen to add the text to the purchased Fancywork label.

You can also purchase packages that contain one or more preprinted fabric labels. Styles of labels range from cute to classic. All you do is fill in the important information, color the label with permanent pens if desired, and attach the label to your quilt.

Heidi Hoff Wurst of Design Plus offers more than two dozen designs of permanently colored labels that are made using a special wax thermal-printing process. This process produces a wonderful surface to write on with permanent markers, pens, or fabric paint. Her Patchwork Care labels give specific washing instructions for quilts, and she also makes custom labels to your specifications.

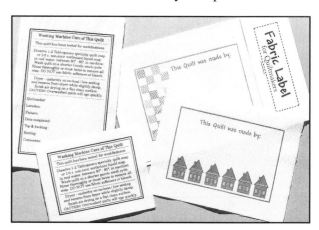

Design Plus labels

Be on the lookout for these and other ready-made labels in quilt shops and quilting-supply catalogs, or check the resource section on pages 59–61 to order by mail directly from the designers.

Some quilts seem to need a label that is not as "high-tech" as a preprinted or a computer-generated design. For an antique quilt or a new quilt made with reproduction fabrics, you might find that a label made from a vintage, hand-embroidered furniture scarf or a lace-edged doily would be more in keeping with the style of the quilt. Look for these in antique shops, or ask friends and family if they have any they would be willing to part with. Use one as a foundation to embroider or write your text on, and apply it as a label to the back of your quilt.

Look also for dated manufacturer's labels that identify new fabrics as reproductions of recognizable fabrics from an earlier period. These labels are often promotional items and are not always available, but they are fun when you can find them. These labels are especially nice if you are making an entire quilt using only reproduction fabrics from one collection. They will let anyone who is interested in the origins of your quilt know that it was made in the late twentieth or early twenty-first century, rather than the period of the fabric style. This will be important information to future quilt historians, especially if you are making a serious effort to re-create an older quilt. Check with the store where you purchased the fabric to see if they have any of these labels, or call the marketing director of the fabric manufacturer to see if labels are available for the collection you are using. Maybe if enough of us ask for these labels, fabric manufacturers will begin to routinely provide them for reproduction fabrics.

Manufacturer's labels

Antique furniture scarves, some of them trimmed with lace, and doilies make lovely frames for label text.

Inked Labels

Using permanent ink to write, draw designs, and color on fabric is an easy way to make wonderful labels. They can be simple or ornate, depending only on the limits of your imagination. Because I am not especially artistic, I use all the help I can find to create label designs.

The easiest labels to make by hand require only a scrap of fabric and a permanent marking pen. You will probably find, however, that even this simple task can be made easier by using some simple tricks and a little practice. Designing your label on paper, even after you become proficient at writing on fabric, allows you to experiment with size and placement of both the text and graphics before transferring it to your fabric.

Choose 100% cotton fabric for labels, rather than polyester-cotton blends, to reduce the chance of the ink bleeding as you write. Choose light-colored solids or subtle prints to make your lettering as visible as possible. A light fabric from your quilt top is usually a good choice.

If you have a light fabric, but the print is too strong, try the wrong side of the fabric. It may give you just the right color, without the distraction of the pattern.

There are pros and cons to washing label fabric; some favor it and others don't. Prewashing fabric removes the sizing, so the inks will penetrate the fibers and last longer. It also makes the fabric softer and more difficult to write on, so you will probably need to stabilize it. If you use starch or sizing as a stabilizer, it will make the fabric easier to write on and seems to reduce the ink's bleeding, but the starch will also block some of the ink from penetrating, and the inked information won't last as long.

Stabilizing fabric with freezer paper makes it easier to write on but more difficult to see through for tracing designs. Freezer paper, sold in the supermarket, is white paper coated on one side with plastic. You can fuse it to fabric, but it can be easily peeled off. It can also be reused several times. Fuse the shiny side of a piece of freezer paper to the wrong side of your fabric. Be sure to iron both sides, using a medium to hot setting, to fuse the paper and fabric together with no air pockets. Experiment with the heat of your iron to get a secure bond. If it's too hot, the plastic coating will melt too much and not stick well. If it's too cool, it will not melt enough and will not stick at all.

Betty Bakie & Christine Davis used black and colored permanent marking pens to add hand-drawn embellishments to their labels.

Freezer paper is especially helpful for freehand writing and drawing. If you are tracing a design and it is difficult to see through the fabric for tracing, use a light table, or tape the fabric to a window over the design you want to trace.

For best results when spraying any kind of sizing or starch to stabilize fabric, wait thirty to sixty seconds after spraying to allow the sizing or starch to completely penetrate the fabric before you iron it dry. Use several light applications, pressing completely dry between each one. Spray and press on the back of the fabric, or use a press cloth to prevent unwanted shine.

Because most of the new permanent inks have not been around long enough for us to really know what they will do chemically to the fabrics that we use them on, we are taking a chance that some of our labels may disintegrate at some future time. For that reason, it makes sense to make a separate label that can be replaced if the inks begin to destroy the label fabric. If you want to avoid this potential problem, use permanent India ink and a stick pen, which can be found in art-supply stores. India ink was used on many antique quilts, and it seems to be a safe way to document your treasures. It takes practice to control India ink with a stick pen, but the viscosity of the ink prevents it from flowing well from a conventional pen.

Most quilting sources suggest Micron Pigma pens as reliable permanent marking pens for lettering, and they are often available in quilt shops. However, there are many other pens available. New pens with different point types and sizes appear in the stores frequently. Don't be afraid to try some that are not listed here. Check out the fine-art and crafts stores in your area if your quilt shop does not carry a large selection of fabric markers. Be on the lookout for pens that claim to be waterproof or permanent and give them a try. It is fun to experiment! Just be sure to always test new brands to see how they work on the fabric you plan to use and to be sure they won't wash out if you use them on a label that will be laundered.

A varied selection of pens can represent a sizable investment, so store them horizontally in airtight plastic bags to keep them from drying out. Be sure to read the instructions that come with the pens because some require heat setting (fifteen seconds with a hot, dry iron), some do not, and some require curing time.

Mimi Dietrich traced her label from one of Kim Churbuck's designs.

The following are several brands I enjoy using.

- **Micron Pigma** pens by Sakura come in nine colors and a choice of fine-line points in six sizes, ranging from a very fine .005 to a broader .08. The brush point for drawing also comes in nine colors. The graphic point comes in four colors with a choice of three tip sizes; and the Calli-Pen for calligraphy comes in six colors but only one tip size. The browns are especially nice for antique-looking labels.

- **Gelly Roll** pens by Sakura are rollerball pens that make a very fine line. They do not bleed into the fabric even if you write slowly. Because of the rollerball, they work better when used on stabilized fabric.

- **Y & C FabricMate** pens by Yasutomo & Co. are ink pens that you use somewhat like fabric paint. They come with either a brush tip or a broad, chisel tip for large designs. They are available in twenty-nine colors and state that the ink is permanent after twenty-four hours. However, five washings in Tide detergent showed some color loss.

- **Y & C Permawriter II** by Yasutomo & Co. is a good pen for writing text and comes in sizes .01 Extra Fine, .03 Fine, and .05 Medium with black ink, as well as a medium tip with brown ink.

- **Marvy Fabric Markers** by Uchida are felt-tipped, permanent on fabric, and come in twelve colors. These are great for filling in color on designs because the ink does not bleed. Heat setting is not required.

- **Regular Marvy Markers** by Uchida, which include the Le Plume pens, come in seventy-five different colors, including translucent pastels. Each pen has both an extra-fine point and a brush point. However, they are not permanent, so use them only for projects that will not be laundered.

- **Sharpie Permanent Markers** by Sanford are readily available anywhere school and office supplies are sold. These pens come in black and several colors, but they are not intended for use on fabric, and the medium and fine-point pens bleed if you write slowly. I often use a black Sharpie ultra-fine point pen for marking lines on freezer paper. Its point is about the same size as the Micron Pigma size .08.

- **ZIG Textile Markers** by Kuretake Co., Ltd., come in several colors. Each pen has a fine point and a brush tip.

- **Identi-pens** by Sakura have two sizes of felt marking points and are marketed as laundry markers, so they should be permanent. However, after washing several times, they do show some fading. They are available in seven colors.

- **Fabric Painters Opaque Markers** by Hunt are actually fabric paint rather than ink. They come in sixteen brilliant colors, and the white shows up well on dark fabrics. They come with either a fine or a medium tip. They are easy to work with and are permanent after heat setting.

- Beautiful fabric-covered, permanent pens by Design Plus come in several colors. These pens are recommended for use with Design Plus labels, which have a special coating, but not for plain fabric.

If you need a colored marking pen that will wash out of fabric (for label designs or for marking quilting patterns), use markers that are clearly labeled "washable." Always pretest these markers on your fabrics to make sure they will wash out.

You may be more comfortable writing on fabric if you have guidelines to help you keep your letters straight. It is easy to use a rotary ruler to mark lines on the paper side of the piece of freezer paper before ironing it to your label fabric.

If you find it difficult to see the drawn lines once the fabric is fused to the freezer paper, try putting a sheet of clean white typing paper or computer paper underneath, especially if you are working on a dark desktop.

If you still can't see the lines, you can use the "tape it to the window or TV screen" trick, but because I can't control my lettering very well on a vertical surface, I would rather use a light table. Check with your local quilt shop or refer to the resource section on pages 59–61 for mail-order sources to purchase a light table, or you can make a simple one yourself.

Your dining room table or even your washing machine can be made into a light table with a piece of glass or Plexiglas and a lamp. My favorite lamp is the Ott-Lite because of its maneuverability and full-spectrum bulb (see "Resources" on page 60). Your empty washing machine is just the right height, and if the dryer is next to the washer, it will help support any extra fabric if you are marking a quilt top. *Make sure the washer is dry inside to avoid electric shock.*

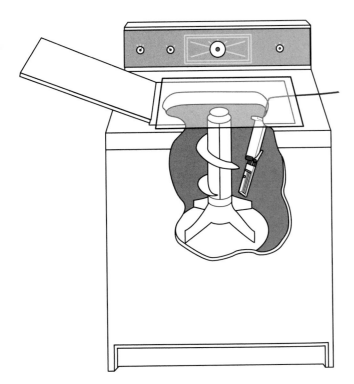

If you have an acrylic extension table for your sewing machine or serger, an Ott-Lite or a fluorescent light stick from the hardware store will make it into a great light table.

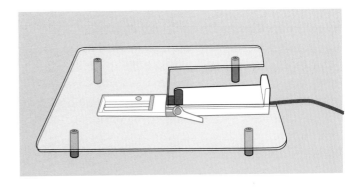

For simple, handwritten labels, you can print the text or use your own cursive handwriting. To embellish your handwriting, copy a font from a design book or use a font from a computer printout. (A "font" is a set of letters and numbers in a particular style.) You don't need to study calligraphy in order to make beautiful handwritten labels. In fact, it is preferable that your writing, especially your own signature, be recognizable. You can easily dress up your handwriting by adding curlicues or flourishes and shading it by making some of the down strokes slightly darker with an extra pen stroke. Practice writing on a scrap of fabric to get the feel of using light strokes to prevent the pen from snagging on the fabric.

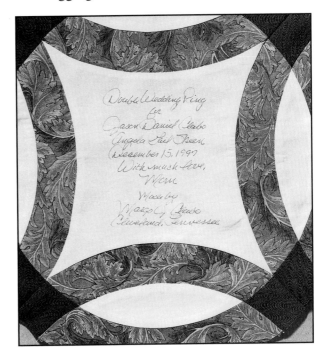

If you don't like the way your own handwriting looks, you can trace letters from alphabets available in copy-art books, or compose your text on a computer and trace the letters from a printout. Because there are hundreds of styles of letters available these days, choosing just the right font may be the most difficult decision you have to make.

If you want graphic designs as well as text on your labels and are not comfortable drawing your own, you can also trace these. Books of label designs to trace or copy onto fabric are available.

Design books for embellishing garments and craft items, though not especially geared toward quilters, offer graphic designs and fonts that you can trace for labels.

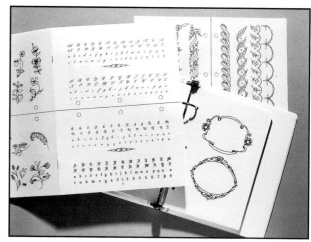

Susan McKelvey's book Limitless Labels to Trace *has designs printed on a special easy-to-see-through paper, and her* Scrolls & Banners to Trace *has designs on heavy paper that are easy to trace.*

Books of embroidery designs and other graphic designs

Sometimes, a quilt-pattern designer will provide wonderful labels to trace that are specially designed to go with particular quilts.

The Critters Quilt Book *by Brandywine Design includes these delightful label designs to trace for the back of your "critters" quilt.*

Be on the lookout for greeting cards, coloring books, art books, newspaper ads, computer clip art, and lots of other graphics for inspiration. **Remember that it is all right for you to copy a design for your own personal use, but you will be violating federal copyright laws if you make multiple copies or use the design in any way for financial gain without written permission. If you are making a project that will be shown publicly,** *never* **use someone else's design without permission.**

The easiest method for tracing a design is to position the fabric over the design you want to trace, tape it in place, and use your permanent marking pens to lightly outline the design. If you are using freezer paper, you will probably need a light table. Trace the outlines of the design, then go back and add the details and colors. Some quilt-label design books provide instructions for coloring in the designs with permanent pens.

The graphics in Kim Churbucks's books are printed on paper that works well for tracing with a light table. You will find a line drawing of Kim's design on page 56. The original label by Kim Churbuck was colored with Pigma Brush pens.

25

To make several labels using the same design, first trace it on the paper side of freezer paper. After the first label is inked and heat-set, just peel the paper off, fuse it to the next piece of fabric, and you are ready to trace again! Remember that if it is a directional design or if it includes lettering, you must reverse the original image before you trace it onto the freezer paper. Turn the original design over and trace it from the back. If it is difficult to see, go over the outline on the back of the original using a light table, or you can have the design reversed at your local copy shop for a nominal fee. You can also reduce or enlarge a design with a copy machine.

If none of these suggestions works and you are still having trouble seeing through your fabric to trace a design, try using a tracing paper for decorative crafts or one of the products that dressmakers use to transfer marks onto garment fabrics. Some new dressmaker's carbons disappear after twenty-four hours.

Saral Transfer Paper works like carbon paper, but needs to be washed out of the fabric. Place the paper over your fabric, with the design on top; then, using a stylus (ball-point pen, pencil, tracing wheel, etc.), follow the outline of your design. These wax-free lines will wash out of fabric, but the design can be inked or painted over with no skipping or bleeding.

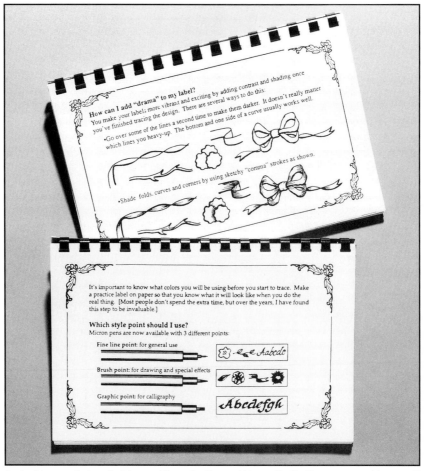

Judy Hoever's books Name That Quilt *and* Your Quilt Deserves a Name *(Patches, Inc.) give good coloring tips and instructions for writing on fabric.*

26

Another way to create several copies of a design easily is to use an iron-on transfer pen. Trace a design onto typing or tracing paper using this special pen, then iron the traced design onto your fabric. You can make several copies with a single application of the ink. Remember, you will need to work from the back of the original if you want to prevent the final image from being reversed.

If you are not comfortable drawing or tracing designs, you can use a preprinted iron-on transfer and color the design with marking pens. Books containing transfers are available in bookstores and crafts-supply stores.

After you have finished the lettering and graphics on your label, heat-set the ink with a hot (cotton setting), dry iron. Use a clean sheet of white typing or computer paper as a blotter over the inked fabric to prevent smeared ink on the fabric or on your iron, especially if you are trying out a new brand of pen. If you used freezer paper to stabilize the fabric, remove it before the paper has cooled while the plastic coating is still soft. Do not start in one corner to pull off the paper, because pulling along the bias may distort the fabric. Separate along the grain line, from the top of the page to the bottom. If the label does cool before you remove the freezer paper, pressing it again to soften it will prevent any distortion in the lettering as you separate the fabric from the paper.

I hope that this chapter has given you some ideas and inspiration for making simple inked labels for your quilts. As you get more comfortable with the concept, I think you will be eager to try some of the more complicated techniques.

Using an iron-on transfer pen

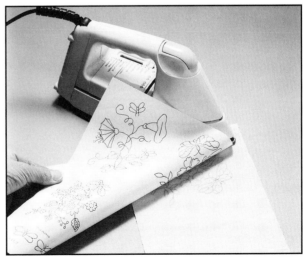
Ready-made transfer designs are easy to find.

Kerry Smith hand printed information about the technique she used to make her quilt and surrounded the label block with a block left over from the quilt top and a piece of flamingo fabric—her "signature."

Margo traced this label design from Little Quilts All Through the House *by Alice Berg, Mary Ellen Von Holt, and Sylvia Johnson.*

A design from Kim Churbuck's The Family Album of Quilt Labels, *traced and colored with permanent pens, labels a quilt for a golfing friend or relative.*

AN ANTIQUE QUILT
Laura Chapman, owner
1932
Charleston, South Carolina
78" x 78"

When Laura first spotted the initials and date appliquéd into the border of this antique quilt, her heart skipped a beat. Although it was only initials and a year, it made her feel connected to the lady who created this lovely work of art. Laura drafted a label design on paper, then traced it onto fabric stabilized with freezer paper, using a black .05 Pigma pen. You will find her design ready for you to trace on page 57.

PINK LEMONADE
by Shelby Morris
1995
Cartersville, Georgia
62" x 80"

Shelby's "Pink Lemonade" was made as a sample quilt for Oxmoor House. She was required to make a quilt using 6"-square Shoo Fly blocks and came up with the unusual setting by adding different colored borders to the blocks. Her label is a delightful appliqué design that is representational of the quilt's name. The large text was machine satin-stitched with black thread, and the small text was handwritten with a permanent pen. (Released by special permission from Sew Many Quilts, Oxmoor House. To order a pattern, call (800) 526-5111.)

BIRD OF PARADISE
by Alice Trach
1996
Ooltewah, Tennessee
78" x 90"

A picture of an antique quilt in *A Treasury of Antique Quilts* inspired Alice to create her beautiful reproduction. She made a few changes from the original design and added a wonderful label by appliquéing duplicate motifs from the front of the quilt that have her name and the date hand embroidered on them. The original quilt top, a Gift of the Trustees, is in the collection of the Museum of American Folk Art in New York. It was created in the vicinity of Albany, New York, between 1858 and 1863, but the maker is unknown.

TIME, LOVE AND TENDERNESS; THE MICHAEL BOLTON QUILT
by Meg Parmaei
1997
Talledega, Alabama
64" x 64"

Meg was inspired by the cover of one of Michael Bolton's albums to create the appliquéd image of him for the center of the quilt. She was able to obtain actual signatures of Michael and all of his band members and backup singers at various events, including one of the softball games that Michael hosts to raise money for the Michael Bolton Foundation, whose mission it is to support women and children at risk. The fabric photo transfers around the border were all pictures that Meg has taken of Michael. Meg plans to donate any prize money the quilt wins to the Michael Bolton Foundation. Meg created the label by typing the text on her typewriter and adding a border.

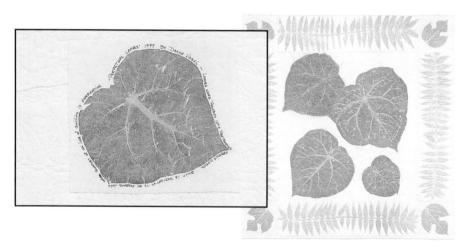

PERPETUAL LEAVES
by Donna Vogel
1997
Chattanooga, Tennessee
49" x 49"

When Donna decided to create a quilt with fresh leaves pounded into the fabric, she recruited her husband to do the pounding. The text of the pounded label is handwritten around the leaf with a Pigma pen.

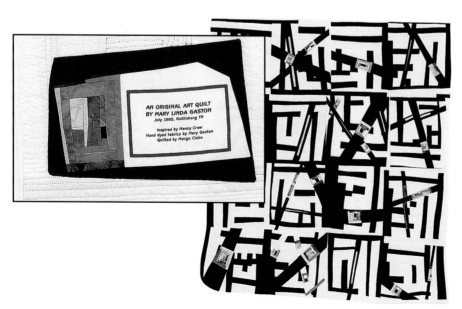

AN ORIGINAL ART QUILT
by Mary Gaston
1995
Gatlinburg, Tennessee
80" x 80"

Mary combined black-and-white fabrics with her own hand-dyed fabrics to create a graphic, contemporary wall quilt. Some of the colored scraps were combined with computer text to make a label that echoes the style of the design on the front of the quilt.

BOBBY'S QUILT
by Lynne Demeter
1996
Cleveland, Tennessee
54" x 62"

This masculine plaid quilt, with Lynne's favorite pieced binding, was made for her husband's fiftieth birthday with half-square triangle blocks. Lynne created the border of the label on her computer with EQ3 software and printed it out, then added the text with her Bernina 1530 sewing machine using Sulky's Tear-Easy stabilizer.

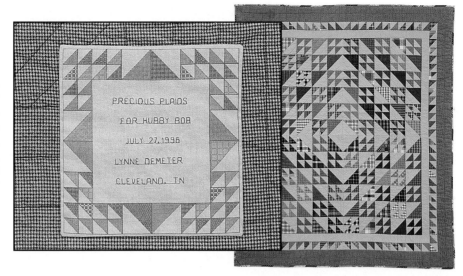

SCRAPPY PATCHES
by Margo J. Clabo
1995
Cleveland, Tennessee
68" x 59"

This quilt is the result of a fabric exchange by the Crazy Quilters of Chattanooga, Tennessee. The label was created by printing the text in DJ Signpost, a font from D. J. Inkers' software, then hand tracing an enlarged design from *All New! Copy Art for Quilters,* coloring it with an assortment of permanent markers, and adding a simple, framing border.

TWELVE DAYS OF CHRISTMAS
by Judith C. Pitts
1997
Ooltewah, Tennessee
62" x 80"

The same year our quilting group made "Quilting Friends Are Sew Special" for me, we also made the blocks for Judy's Christmas quilt. We used the packaged patterns for the "Twelve Days of Christmas," an original design by Linda Hohag of Brandywine Design pattern company. For this great label, Judy printed the text on the label fabric with her computer and added the border fabric. Then she reduced the size of the Partridge in a Pear Tree block pattern and fused the pieces with Aleene's Hot Stitch fusible web. She secured the edges with a satin stitch, using Sulky's Tear-Easy stabilizer.

31

A TIME FOR REFLECTING
by Donna Vogel
1996
Chattanooga, Tennessee
42" x 60"

Donna's original art quilt depicts the Tennessee River. The text for her beautiful label was created in Print Artist software. The irises were fused in place with Trans-Web fusible bond, and the three-dimensional trilliums and leaves were made from two layers of fabric fused together with Trans-Web.

LES POMMES
by Candace Tucker
1997
White Pine, Tennessee
35½" x 54½"

Les pommes is French for "the apples." This award-winning original art quilt was created for a guild challenge and uses a technique Candace read about in an article by Sheri Wood in *Threads* magazine (Nov. '96, No. 67). The label's original apple design was drawn with a Sharpie Ultra Fine Permanent marker onto fabric stabilized with freezer paper, and the text was written freehand. The quilt is now owned by Pete and Linda Claussen.

DIONAEA
by Jill Hoevel Bryant
1996
St. Peters, Missouri
61" x 61"

Dionaea muscipula is the Latin name for Venus's-flytrap. Jill made this quilt for the New Quilts from Old Favorites competition, sponsored by the American Quilter's Society. The theme for 1997 was Mariner's Compass quilts. Jill used paper piecing for the compass and the border of this original design. She created the label for her quilt by painting the text with a Speedball Painter Opaque Paint Marker and adding a striking, striped border, which she trimmed at a rakish angle.

TWO MINUTES IN MAY
by Shirley P. Kelly
1995
Colden, New York
78" x 40"

This award-winning quilt has appeared in several publications, but most people never get to see the back of the quilt. Shirley says that "All of my quilts are reversible, so I feel that the label should be as attractive as the back and fit into the motif of the back. A great deal of time goes into their design and execution, as my quilts portray an important event, and the label is used to further the facts. Because my hand-appliquéd competition quilts take approximately two years to complete, the time spent on their labels is time well spent." On this label, Shirley cross-stitched the Twin Spires of Churchill Downs, the track depicted in the quilt.

JAGUAR
by Joshua Troy Clabo
1995
Cleveland, Tennessee
41" x 32"

My youngest son, Joshua, made this wall hanging when he was 18 years old. He enlarged the outline of the car from a photograph in *Classic Cars* magazine (April '95, pages 67–68) and added details such as the spokes of the wheel with machine stitches. He made the label in the shape of the Jaguar logo on the front of the quilt and used a computer for the text. (*Classic Cars* is published by IPC Magazines, Ltd., London, England.)

AUNT BERYL'S GARDEN
by Amy Chamberlin
1996
Plano, Texas
53" x 58"

This award-winning tribute to Amy's Aunt Beryl showcases a sewing technique that Amy has been teaching since the late 1970s. She uses tiny circles of many different thread colors to create beautiful portraits. For the label of this quilt, Amy used Graphics 2000 Photo Transfer Service to transfer the photo of Aunt Beryl and the printed text of the label to a piece of fabric, and appliquéd it to the quilt back. All of the cursive text was done freehand with a zigzag satin stitch over a tissue-paper draft of the letters. I am still amazed!

QUILTING FRIENDS ARE SEW SPECIAL
by Margo J. Clabo
1996
Cleveland, Tennessee
72" x 53½"

In 1996, a special group of quilting friends asked each member what kind of quilt she wanted the group to make for her. This was my choice. I had always loved Carol Doak and Sherry Reis's quilt "Forever Friends," on the cover of Carol's book *Quiltmaker's Guide: Basics & Beyond,* because it reminds me of quilting friendships. Because I am a machine quilter, I changed the design by adding the "seamstress," another paper-cut design by Alison Cosgrove Tanner of "Papercuttings by Alison." The label is a large-scale pieced block; a computer was used to add the text and to scan the silhouette image.

COUNTRY SONGBIRD
by Margo J. Clabo
1996
Cleveland, Tennessee
93" x 108"

I was commissioned by Gina and Steve Owen to create this quilt, which is on display in their shop, Gina's Bernina Sewing Center, in Knoxville, Tennessee. The design is the "Country Songbird Quilt," ©1990 by Good Books, Intercourse, Pennsylvania, and is used by permission. The label design was created by scanning a drawing of the quilt layout from the pattern into the computer and adding text. After the label was printed, the design was hand colored with permanent pens to match the colors of the quilt top.

EASTERN INFLUENCE
by Susan Tennill
1996
Springfield, Virginia
74½" x 98"

Susan combined patterns from several sources to create this wonderful quilt. The Noshi pattern is by Marge Burkell; the wild flower patterns are by Sweet Memories Publishing Co. (Virginia Athey, owner and distributor); the fans are from the book *Changing Seasons,* by Penguin, USA; and the Asian girls are the Myomi pattern by Amy Myoraku. The text on her label was created with a sewing machine on fabric stabilized with Stitch & Ditch. She added some silk-ribbon embroidery and framed the label with Bow Tie blocks.

AUTUMNAL SHADOWS
by Margo J. Clabo
1992
Cleveland, Tennessee
56" x 70"

A small, computer-generated label tells where this quilt, the state winner for Tennessee in the second All-American Quilt Contest, has traveled. A larger label records the basics in computer-generated text on a piece of my own hand-dyed fabric. Selected motifs from the quilt's backing fabric, fused with Trans-Web, form a frame in the middle of black background fabric. The edges of the fused pieces are zigzagged with YLI brand smoky-colored nylon thread. I used white Trash Paper from a drafting-supply store as a stabilizer.

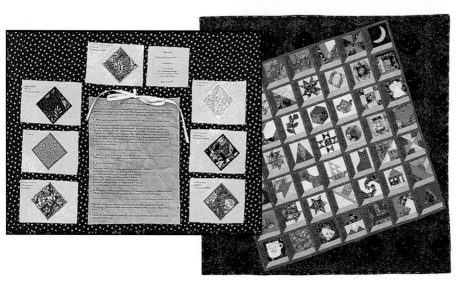

FRIENDS FAR AND NEAR
by Cathy Long
1997
Clinton, Tennessee
51" x 51"

When Cathy and six of her friends decided to make friendship quilts, Cathy began a journal of the experience. All seven of the quilters used the same blocks to create completely different quilts. Cathy's multiple labels not only show the fabric that each quilter contributed, but the large label, which was created with a computer to record the rules of the block exchange, is actually a pocket to keep the journal in! She said that she did not want to forget the details of making this quilt with special friends.

ROSS'S QUILT
by Laura Chapman
1995
Charleston, South Carolina
11½" x 11½"

Paper-piecing blocks, sold in a kit by Great Lengths Quilt Shop in Skyland, North Carolina (now closed), were the basis for this cute wall quilt that Laura made for her son, Ross. The delightful label was simply made by cutting cats from the border fabric and fusing them to background fabric. The text was handwritten with a permanent pen, and the "quilting" around the edges was also done with a pen.

SOMAR SOLVERV (SUNBURST)
by Tone Haugen-Cogburn
1996
Maryville, Tennessee
36" x 36"

This award-winning original design features a handwritten label with a pieced border. Tone is Norwegian, and she says that the title of the quilt translates literally to "summer solstice," but she thinks the quilt conveys a sunburst feeling.

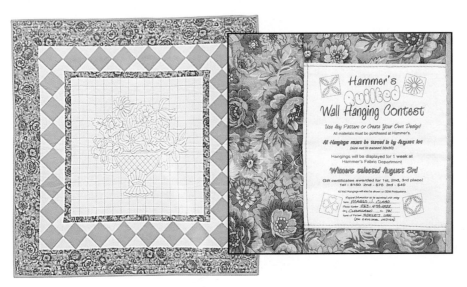

HAMMER'S QUILT
by Margo J. Clabo
1996
Cleveland, Tennessee
29" x 29"

A challenge issued by Hammer's Department Store in Winchester, Tennessee, resulted in this wall hanging. The label was made by scanning the store's entry form for the quilt contest into my computer and printing it onto the label fabric.

36

Embellished Labels

The most obvious embellishments for labels are pieced or appliquéd components copied from the front of the quilt. I was surprised to learn that one of the prettiest labels I have ever seen was placed on the back of a finished quilt to cover an unsightly stain that had happened during quilting. The stain could not be removed, so the quiltmaker used it as an excuse to create a very large, elaborate, appliquéd label that beautifully complemented the front of the quilt!

The label is a great place to include a small sample of your other crafting hobbies. And the sky is the limit for embellishing your labels—anything goes. If you enjoy plain embroidery or silk-ribbon embroidery, cross-stitching, thread painting, silk screening, stenciling, or beading, use the label to show off your talents. A label is a small project, and it can make a quilt uniquely yours.

Beaded label on hand-marbled fabric by Pat Keran of Signal Mountain, Tennessee

A sailboat motif cut from a novelty print provided a clever place to inscribe identifying information on Sandy Turner's quilt.

Appliqué

Appliqué is an easy way to make the quilt label relate to the design of the quilt. If the quilt design is appliquéd, you can simply repeat the design on the label and add text. If the quilt is a pieced design that includes a fabric with distinctive motifs, you can appliqué one of the motifs to the label. Use your favorite method of hand or machine appliqué.

If you do not enjoy appliqué work, consider using fusible web to attach your motif. Judy's "Twelve Days of Christmas" label (page 31), Donna's "A Time for Reflecting" label (page 32), and Margo's "Autumnal Shadows" label (page 35) were all attached using fusible web.

Follow the manufacturer's directions to prepare the appliqué motif with the fusible web. After fusing the motif to the prepared text fabric, secure the edges with decorative stitches or nylon thread, using a narrow zigzag stitch. This step is not necessary if you use HeatnBond Ultra, which will secure the motif, but this fusible will also make your label somewhat stiff.

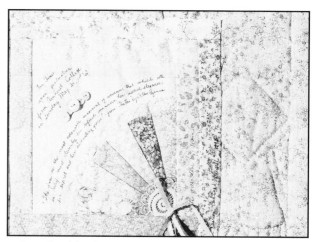

A lacy fan block is appliquéd to the back of Aimee Newell's quilt.

Embroidery

Embroidery has long been the method of choice for labeling quilts. If you enjoy this type of handwork, simply embroider your name, date, city, and any additional information on the backing fabric before you make your quilt sandwich. Any stitch will work: chain stitch, running stitch, outline stitch, French knots, or satin stitch. Silk ribbon or other embroidered embellishments can also be added to labels with text that was printed using other techniques. Judy Pitts added these beautiful flowers and the outline stitch around computer-generated text.

Laura Reinstatler fused and stitched a bouquet of motifs cut from a rose print to the backing fabric of her quilt. Then, she drew a vase and added the inscription with a permanent marking pen.

Silk-ribbon embroidery by Judy Pitts of Ooltewah, Tennessee

For a very simple label, Judy hand embroidered just her initials and the year.

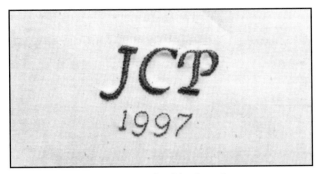

A simple monogram stitched by hand

Cross-stitching

There is a really great way of making perfectly embroidered cross-stitches without marking on your label fabric. Purchase a piece of waste canvas a little larger than the area you want to embroider. (Waste canvas looks much like Penelope needle-point canvas, except that every tenth thread is blue for ease in counting.)

Chart your text on graph paper. Baste the canvas to the label fabric and work your cross-stitch design over the starchy threads of the canvas.

After completing the embroidery, soak the stitched area in tepid water to rinse away the starch, then carefully remove the basting and canvas threads. Almost like magic, you will have perfect cross-stitches with no evidence remaining as to how you did it. Judy added Sunbonnet Sue to muslin that was preprinted with computer-generated text.

If you prefer to use Aida cloth for your label, the design can be simple or complex. (Also see Shirley Kelly's cross-stitched label on page 33.)

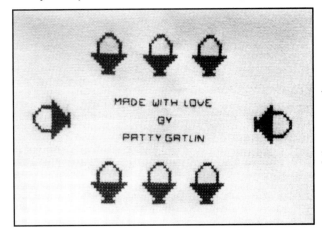

Cross-stitched baskets by Patty Gatlin of Cleveland, Tennessee

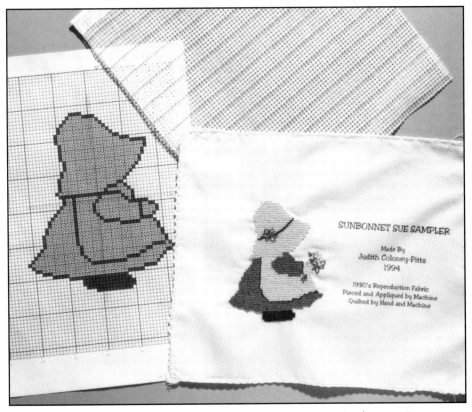

Waste canvas is removed after cross-stitching your pattern. Sunbonnet Sue label by Judy Pitts of Ooltewah, Tennessee.

Using Signature Fabric

There are many ways to approach making a label for a quilt: relating the label to the design on the front, the name of the quilt, the occasion for its creation, the name of the recipient—all of these are options. Consider also the idea of using a "signature" fabric on *all* of your quilt labels no matter what approach you take. If there is a fabric with a particular pattern, color, or design motif that you like to use and identifies you, including that signature fabric or motif on the label could be a special way to say this quilt was made by you.

I often use this quilter's silhouette from Paper Cuttings by Alison (used here by permission) as a "signature" motif on my labels.

Stenciling

Stenciling is an easy way to transfer a design to fabric. Many stencil designs lend themselves well to creating quilt labels. The design can be outlined and colored in with permanent pens, or it can be stenciled in the traditional way with stenciling paint or paint crayons and a stenciling brush.

Sample labels by Gladys Grace of Pomfret Center, Connecticut. Gladys provides stenciling instructions with each stencil you purchase from her. She recommends that you use her paints and brushes, and if you see her booth at a quilt show, be sure to stop by for a free hands-on demonstration! These are copyrighted designs; do not reproduce them.
JD Stencils and Paint Crayons by Plaid (below). Stenciled label by Daryleen Noble of Cerritos, California.

Stamped Designs

A wide selection of rubber stamps is available, and these can be used to make attractive labels. Please check "Resources" on pages 59–61. If you like to "surf the web," you will find lots of information and supply sources for rubber stamping.

Some stamps are complete quilt labels or quilt blocks. All you have to add is color and text to the stamped outlines. A stamp that forms a border works well for labels.

Pelle's Stamps are clear acrylic so you can see where you are stamping.

Try rubber stamps with shaded designs, such as this strawberry by Rubber Stampede. Translucent markers, such as the pastels by Marvy, allow the shading on the stamped image to show through the colored ink, but these markers are not permanent, so use them on labels that will not be laundered.

A stamp with shading in the image can be colored with fabric markers.

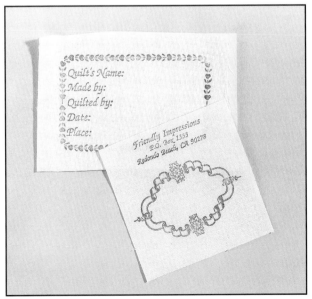

Friendly Impressions has rubber stamps that make great label designs.

I use Deka or ZimPrints Permanent Acrylic fabric paints, or Fabrico, a water-based, fabric-ink stamp pad, for creating stamped designs on labels.

Stamped label by Jan Smiley of Fort Mill, South Carolina. Jan created this beautiful label with ZimPrints stamps and computer-designed text on her batik fabric.

For best results, prewash and dry light-colored cotton fabrics before you apply ink or paint to them. Some of these designs are beautiful without embellishment, but it is fun to add color with permanent pens, fabric crayons, or fabric paint and to personalize the designs with text.

Nanette Rebori of ZimPrints, Inc., provides the following instructions for rubber stamping on fabric. Before stamping on your label, practice on a scrap of fabric.

1. Smooth your fabric over a piece of cardboard or other hard surface. A large square of felt underneath will provide an extra cushion for thinner fabrics. Occasionally, a little paint will bleed through the fabric, so use some newsprint or kraft paper to protect your stamping surface. If you find that a lot of paint is bleeding through, be careful when you move the fabric around, so that the paint on the protective underlay doesn't rub all over the back of the fabric. I use a giant piece of felt so I can move to a different part of the felt if a lot of paint is bleeding through. The felt absorbs the paint and by the time I've finished stamping over one side of the felt, the other side will be dry.

2. Dip a 1" foam brush into the paint. Paint the stamp surface evenly and generously enough to ensure that you'll get a deep, vivid print. A brayer (a hand-inking roller, available in art-supply stores) works well for spreading paint or ink on stamps. For two colors on one stamped image, paint them *both* onto the stamp before stamping (use different brushes for each color). Practice this, because it is easy to apply a little too much paint. When using acrylic fabric paint, brush the paint onto the stamp smoothly with a light touch in a nice, generous layer. You want the paint to cover the surface only—not fill up the grooves. If you accidentally get paint in a groove, use a toothpick or a cotton swab to wipe it out right away.

3. Press the stamp firmly onto the fabric and lift it straight off. Dry your stamped creation for an hour or so, then heat-set it by ironing on the wrong side of the fabric.

4. Wash the foam brushes and stamps in warm, soapy water, and you're done!

When you use the Fabrico stamp pads, try turning the pad upside down to lightly tap the color onto the stamp surface. This method of inking allows better control over the amount of color on the stamp surface. Fabrico stamp pads are very "juicy," and pressing hard into the pad causes the color to fill up the grooves of the stamp and dribble down the edges. These stamp pads are so juicy, you can also use them with a paintbrush. You might stamp a line-art image onto the fabric with a black Fabrico, then use an artist's brush, dabbed on a colored Fabrico to paint inside the outline.

If you use Deka paint, double-coat the stamp. For the first coat, spread on just the lightest application of paint. Allow that to dry just to tackiness, then re-coat more heavily. This double coating helps cover the stamping surfaces evenly and eliminates bubbling. Sometimes, lightly sanding the stamp with fine sandpaper or an emery board before using it will rough up the stamp surface a bit and help it to accept the paint more easily. ZimPrints fabric paint goes on smoothly the very first time, and it is not necessary to sand your stamp or double-coat it.

Fabrico and Deka and ZimPrints paints all have a "soft hand," meaning you cannot feel the ink or paint on the fabric at all. Heat-set all of these. The best way to do this is to iron the fabric, either upside down or with a press cloth, on the highest setting the fabric will accept. Be sure the ink or paint is dry. Deka and ZimPrints paints dry very quickly; an hour's wait is usually more than enough. Fabrico takes a bit longer.

After heat setting, ZimPrints and Deka paints are permanent and will stay incredibly bright through zillions of washings and even bleaching. Fabrico is permanent, but it does fade or lighten a tiny bit. It is not as vivid as the paints.

All three products are nontoxic and water-soluble. Stamps and brushes can be washed under running water; soap is optional. Set stamps on their ends to dry. Don't soak them for prolonged periods, because the wood can eventually split. The sooner you wash your stamps, the easier it is to clean them! Baby wipes are good for cleaning paint and inks off of acrylic stamps. A toothbrush or nail brush is handy for scrubbing stubborn ink or paint out of grooves.

The product literature says that you can wash out mistakes made with Fabrico. Nanette says that she was able to wash out an image only if she did it immediately, and it required vigorous scrubbing by hand. As a result, she recommends that mistakes be used as opportunities for creativity. She says, "I try to include some small stamps in every design, because they can appear in unexpected places without throwing the whole design off-balance. They usually appear right on top of the place where I dropped a foam brush out of my mouth, onto the fabric. That is what little stars and tiny bug stamps are for."

To use colored markers on rubber stamps, breathe a heavy "haaaaa" on the stamp (like when you clean your eyeglasses) to moisten the ink for a better image.

For more information about stamping, look in the Yellow Pages for rubber-stamping stores in your area. There are also several magazines for stampers, and you can check "Resources" on page 62 for stamping Web sites.

Photo Transfers

If you don't want to draw or trace your completed text or graphics onto fabric or if you want to include a photograph in your label design, a photo-transfer process works well. Using photo-transfer paper, available at many quilt shops and crafts-supply stores, is an extremely easy way to create a fabric label, although it does require the use of a color copy machine. Copy centers and many office-supply stores offer full- or self-service color copying. Shop around for the best price and to find someone who will help you set up the machine for the best color copies.

Any of the following photos would be a great choice to include on a quilt label:

- You working on the quilt

- The student, for a graduation quilt

- The new baby, for a baby quilt

- The new home, for a house-warming quilt

- A group of friends, for a friendship or going-away quilt

- The bride and groom, for a wedding quilt

- The family, for a son or daughter leaving home for college or a job

You don't necessarily have to include a photograph when you use this technique. Text can be generated on a computer and photo-transferred to make it more permanent than if it were printed with a computer printer. Emily Parson of Chicago, Illinois, used this method for the text on this unusual label. Who says labels have to be square? Emily used the font "Whimsy" to create the text on her computer and printed it on a BubbleJet printer onto Canon transfer paper. She then ironed the design onto the white fabric. Because she fused the white snowflake onto the black background fabric, it did not need a stabilizer when she appliquéd it with her sewing machine.

Label by Emily Parson of Chicago, Illinois

Use the method of your choice to design your text and graphics on a sheet of 8½" x 11" paper. You could even start with preprinted stationery.

This Quilt Image stationery by Anita Tinlin of Skills Graphics is available in quilt shops and directly from Skills Graphics. (Stationery design ©1996 by Skills Graphics; Quilt design ©1992 by Little Quilts)

Dot's label incorporates a design from the Quilt Image stationery above.

Take your design to the color copy machine and print it on the transfer paper according to the manufacturer's directions. Be sure to use the "reverse image" feature on the copy machine, or your entire design will be backward! Take the printed design home, and with a hot iron, transfer it to your cotton fabric. Using cotton muslin with a 200-thread count (or higher) will make the image clearer. After the design has been transferred, be sure to reduce the iron temperature to warm before the final press.

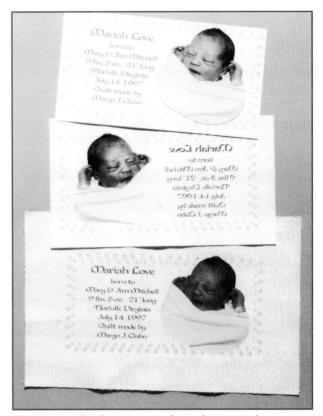

Photo-transfer designs must be color copied as a mirror image.

If you are not interested in doing this process yourself, there are several companies who will transfer photos to fabric for you. See "Resources" on pages 59–61.

Machine-Embroidered Designs

A sewing machine capable of creating decorative stitches and text is a wonderful tool for making fabric quilt labels. Follow your machine's directions for stabilizing your fabric and setting up the program, then let the machine do the work.

Tyna Meers, of Franklin, Tennessee, created this label design for a quilt she made for a friend. She started by printing the text with a computer printer directly on her label fabric, then used the Bernina Deco 500 Embroidery machine to add the horse, with Sulky's Totally Stable tearaway stabilizer behind the embroidered design.

Label design by Tyna Meers of Franklin, Tennessee

Center Yourself

For MiMi, my friend and teacher.
Thank you for your enthusiasm and love of the sport.

Quilted By: Tyna Meers
Date: May 18, 1997
For: MiMi Pantelides, Centered Riding Instructor

Wendy Taylor, of Chattanooga, Tennessee, created the following three wonderful labels. For the first one, she scanned the graphics from *All New! Copy Art for Quilters* and translated them for the sewing machine, using Husqvarna Viking digitizing software. The text and graphics were then stitched with the Husqvarna Viking #1+ sewing machine on fabric stabilized with Jiffy's Tear Away.

Label design by Wendy Taylor of Chattanooga, Tennessee

Wendy also made this label for her nephew's birthday quilt. First, she stitched a tiny quilt pieced from the fabrics on the front of the quilt into place with a wide satin stitch, then she machine embroidered the graphic of the little boy and the text.

Label design by Wendy Taylor of Chattanooga, Tennessee

Wendy used a Viking #1 to create this shadow appliqué design with its pretty flowers and leaves.

Label design by Wendy Taylor of Chattanooga, Tennessee

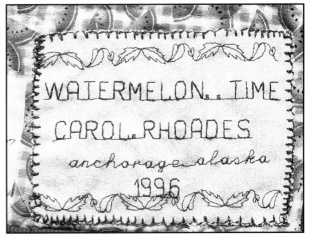

Carol Rhoads stitched this label using her computerized sewing machine.

Typewritten Labels

If you don't own a computer or are uncomfortable using one and you have access to a typewriter, you can easily add text to your label by typing on fabric that has been fused to freezer paper. The text will show up better and be more permanent if you type over each line a second time and heat-set it with a hot, dry iron. Your label can be embellished, or it can simply be a typed recitation of the quilt's history.

You can also type information in the blank area of a label stamped on fabric. Start in the center of the label and back-space for every other letter of a line of text to center it in the available space.

Depending on the typewriter, you will be limited to the style and size of the type; usually a choice of pica (ten characters per inch) or elite (twelve characters per inch).

There are many typewriters still out there, and each one takes a different kind of ribbon or inking system, so make a sample label to see how your brand of ink holds up when washed. If the ink shows signs of fading after you launder it, remove the label before washing the quilt and include that instruction on your label so you won't forget.

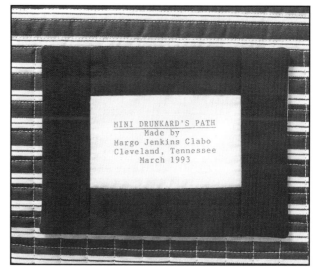

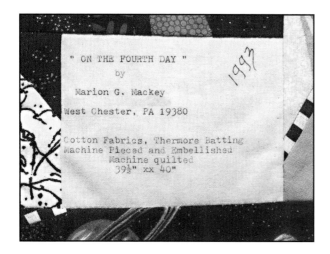

Computer-Aided Designs

The following technique is my favorite for designing and creating labels, but it is not the most permanent method. If your labels will be subjected to repeated washings, such as those on baby quilts or lap quilts, I recommend that you use more permanent techniques, such as stitching, fabric paints and permanent pens, or photo transfers to create your labels. You can still use the computer to design your label, but a computer-printed label will not withstand repeated washings.

Although I have been using a Hewlett Packard DeskJet 600 to print fabric labels for several years and cannot detect any damage to it, please note that *this technique is not recommended by the computer industry.* Fibers, threads, and the bulk of the fabric can damage parts of the printer, so please PROCEED AT YOUR OWN RISK. *The author and the publisher of this book will not be responsible for damage done to your computer printer if you use this method.*

I have never had a fabric label jam in my printer, but I have heard of some that have, so read your manual ahead of time to avoid panic in case of a jam. If your printer allows you to adjust for extra thickness when printing envelopes, try that setting for printing on fabric.

Because computer technology is changing so fast, I will not give information about specific printers or inks. I will just share the information I have gathered in my experiments and research.

The colored inks in most printers are water-soluble, but some black inks are pigments and may be fairly permanent without adding fixatives or pre-treating.

Truly permanent black pigment inks have been difficult to find and use, bacause they tended to clog ink-cartridge jets. New inks flow more easily. They are currently being introduced and should soon be widely available.

FS-101 Fabric Sheets, treated fabric sheets for computer printing, are currently available from Canon and come in a package of 10 sheets, each 9½" x 14". You may have to trim them for your printer. The fabric sheets have been pretreated with a fixative, but each package also contains a packet of dry fixative that you mix with water so you can soak the printed sheet to further ensure the image will be permanent. Test this fixative solution before you use it on your entire printed sheet. The sheets are expensive, but so is taking your image to a copy shop to have it transferred to fabric.

If your project will not be washed, you can print wonderful, colorful images on untreated fabric. Use 100% cotton fabric, 200-thread count or higher, for the best-quality images. Light colors work best; however, tone-on-tone fabrics (even light ones) that have a design painted on the surface do not generally work well. If you want to use these fabrics, try printing on the back side. You will still be able to see some design, and the inks will be better able to penetrate the fabric.

1. Fuse the wrong side of the label fabric to the shiny side of a piece of freezer paper with a hot, dry iron. Iron both the fabric side and the paper side to get out all of the air pockets and to securely bond the entire unit. *Make sure that there are absolutely no loose threads, which could severely damage your printer.* I like to gently roll the surface of the fabric with a sticky lint remover to assure myself that no threads remain.

2. Use a rotary cutter to trim the paper-backed fabric to 8½" x 11", 8½" x 14", or a size compatible with your printer. Trimming after fusing reduces the likelihood of loose threads at the edges.

3. Feed the fabric into the printer one sheet at a time face down and print in transparency mode for the brightest colors. Immediately heat-set the computer ink with a hot, dry iron, using a clean sheet of typing or computer paper as a blotter to prevent any ink from transferring to your iron. Heat setting as soon as the fabric comes out of the printer seems to allow maximum penetration of the wet ink into the cotton fibers.

4. Wait 24 hours. Heat-set the label again, using a paper blotter, and while it is still warm, peel the freezer paper from the fabric. Doing this while it is still warm will help prevent the fabric from distorting, because the plastic coating will be soft. Avoid pulling from a corner. Loosen the fabric across the entire top and pull gently to separate it from the paper.

To make your own fabric somewhat colorfast, try the following instructions provided by Melissa Boyd, a crafter and employee of Hewlett Packard's inkjet division.

1. Soak your fabric for 15 minutes in a solution of ½ water, ½ Downy Ultra Free fabric softener. Use only the Downy with no added dyes or fragrances.
2. Rinse well under running water and hang to dry.
3. Iron the fabric, fuse it to freezer paper, then spray thoroughly with Static Guard or other antistatic spray. Dry completely before printing.
4. After printing, spray with a fixative such as Grumbacker Myston Workable Fixative Krylon or Krylon Workable Fixatif, available in art-supply stores. These products contain toxic solvents and must be used with proper ventilation. They are not specifically recommended for this use, so results may vary.

In my experience, some computer inks can be made more permanent by pretreating the label fabric with Retayne, a color fixative for commercially dyed cotton fabrics. Mix 1 teaspoon of Retayne in 1 cup of hot (140°) water. Add the label fabric and let it soak for 20 minutes. Rinse well with cool water and iron dry. Print as described above.

Since computer inks are pigments rather than the textile dyes that Retayne was developed for, Retayne is not guaranteed to prevent fading when used in this manner. Retayne also carries the Cali-

These samples were printed with a Cannon BubbleJet printer. In Sample 1, the fabric on the right was not prewashed or laundered after printing. The fabric on the left was not prewashed and was laundered once. In Sample 2, the fabric on the right was prewashed and pretreated with Retayne. The fabric in the middle was laundered once. The fabric on the left was laundered twice. Pretreating with Retayne caused some change in the color of the fabric. Compare it with the unwashed fabric on the right in Sample 1.

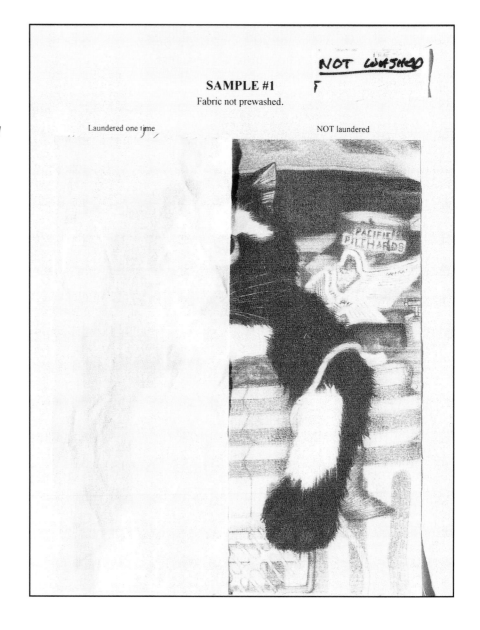

NOT WASHED

SAMPLE #1

Fabric not prewashed.

Laundered one time

NOT laundered

fornia Prop 65 warning label, which means it contains a known cancer-causing chemical, so the manufacturer recommends that you wear rubber gloves when using it.

Some permanence may be obtained by spraying the label with Krylon Workable Fixatif, available in art-supply stores. It contains toxic solvents, however, and must be used with proper ventilation. Note that this product is also not recommended for this use, so results may vary.

I made a number of admittedly unscientific comparison tests. I used DeskJet, LaserJet, BubbleJet, and Dot Matrix printers and an old electric typewriter to test different combinations of processes on forty-five computer-printed pieces of

100% cotton fabric: washed or unwashed, heat-set or not heat-set, treated or untreated with Retayne or Krylon, hand washed with Orvus Paste or machine washed with Tide, and dried flat or machine dried in a hot dryer. Make your own sample labels, using your equipment, and test them for colorfastness.

I found the LaserJet inks to be the blackest, but the others were acceptable. The BubbleJet that I tested faded more than most after washing. Surprisingly, the ink from the old typewriter held up very well after repeated washings. Immediate heat setting with a hot, dry iron helped to set all of the inks. The fixative treatments seemed to set some of the inks but caused others to fade. As I expected, using warm water and Orvus Paste on a gentle cycle and

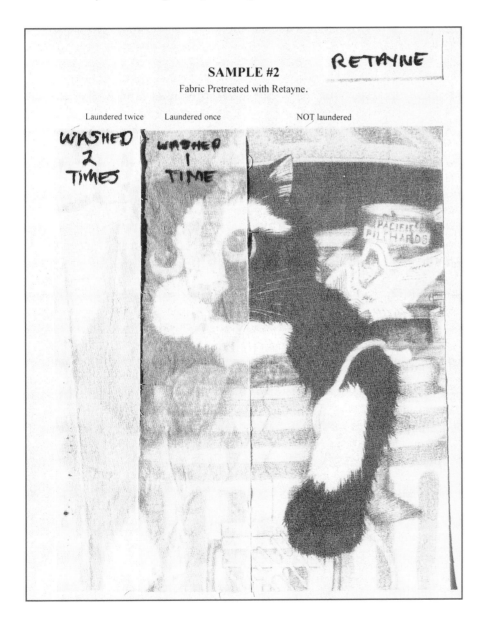

SAMPLE #2
Fabric Pretreated with Retayne.

Laundered twice   Laundered once   NOT laundered

drying a label flat produced better results than harsh detergent and a hot, tumbling dryer. All of the colored inks faded considerably when washed, but they make beautiful labels, so use them if the label won't be laundered. The Retayne pretreatment was especially helpful with colored inks.

If you have a word-processing program on your Mac or PC, you can print your text with any font from your program. Play with the fonts and the size, placement, and spelling of the information before you print it on your fabric. Then add borders or embellishments if desired.

The Scrappy Patches quilt label at right was created by printing the text (D J Signpost by D. J. Inkers) on the label fabric, then tracing an enlarged copy of a rake and fabric squares from *All New! Copy Art for Quilters*. The colors were added by hand with an assortment of colored pens before the border was added. See the quilt on page 31.

There are several software packages on the market now for creating both pieced and appliquéd quilt designs. (See "Resources" on page 62 for a Web site that gives unbiased information about the different quilt software packages.) Some programs even enable you to print out the actual template

The design at the top of this Scrappy Patches label was traced from an enlarged graphic.

shapes on your printer. If you can use one of these programs to design your quilt, you can also use it to design a quilt label. Lynne Demeter, of Cleveland, Tennessee, designed and colored these two labels in EQ3 by The Electric Quilt Company, then exported them to Print Shop to add the text. She found that the crispness and texture definition was much better than when printed directly from EQ3.

Lynne Demeter created these labels with EQ3 and Print Shop software.

Computer Clip Art

Computer clip-art programs include pictures you can use with the software packages already in your computer. These are not graphics programs, but are additional graphics to be added to the programs you are already using. Always check the listed PC or MAC system requirements before you purchase clip art or software packages to make sure that they are compatible with your computer.

This scrappy Patch label was created with QuilText and QuiltBlock Too designs.

Angela's label was created with a predesigned template and a font from Inspirations by D. J. Inkers.

Two original designs by Carolyn Kissel, QuiltClips designer from Raleigh, North Carolina, were composed with Print Master Gold. QuiltClips offers 101 graphics designed especially for quilters.

Scanners

A scanner on your computer provides even more options for graphics on your labels. (Don't forget to respect the copyrights of others; see page 25.) The images used for Olivia's label were scanned into my computer's graphics program from *All New! Copy Art for Quilters*. Because Olivia's hair is longer than the original drawing of the little girl, and her quilt pattern was different from the one in the drawing, I made changes before I scanned the image. After combining the two images, I added the text, printed the label, and hand colored the design.

Lynne Demeter made the label for Bobby's quilt by scanning the paw prints and the small kitty from *All New! Copy Art for Quilters* and the other cat from an old greeting card into the computer and composing the graphics and text. After the design was printed, Lynne added her signature with a black Pigma pen.

Tyna Meers label for her daughter Olivia's quilt.

Lynne's label for Bobby's quilt

The image used for the Country Songbird quilt was scanned into my computer's graphics program from the pattern by Good Books (used by permission). I manipulated it to form a complete border, then added text. I printed the label and added color by hand. See the quilt on page 34.

Donna Vogel made a second label for her quilt (see "A Time for Reflecting" on page 32) using a color scanner to add a photograph of the quilt to the label. It was transported into Print Artist, where she added text and printed it onto the label fabric. Donna's wall quilt will not be laundered, so this wonderful, computer-printed label can be used without worry. For a permanent design, however, a photo-transfer method would be more suitable.

If you want a computer-generated label but do not have the equipment to make one yourself, contact Chosen Sisters Heirloom Labels. They will let you choose from a selection of borders, fonts, and graphics and will create a custom-designed label just for you.

I hope that these labels and techniques will inspire you to create unique labels for your own quilts. You might want to take a few extra minutes at the next quilt show you attend and ask one of the white-gloved hostesses to show you the backs of the quilts. You may find some hidden 'back art' as well as some wonderful labels.

Sew long!

Margo Clabo

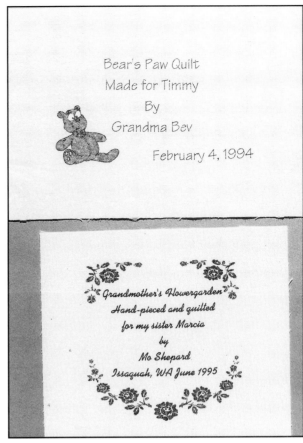

Custom labels by Chosen Sisters

Original design from Country Songbird pattern book.
Country Songbird label.

©Kim Churbuck

Copy Art

Note: The copy art shown here may be reproduced for your personal use only. It is a violation of federal copyright laws to make multiple copies or use these designs in any way for financial gain without written permission from the designer. (To contact the designers, see "Resources" on pages 59–61.)

Original design by Laura Chapman

Bibliography

Berg, Alice, Mary Ellen Von Holt & Sylvia Johnson. *Little Quilts All Through the House*. Bothell, Wash.: That Patchwork Place, 1993.

Buffington, Adriene. *Hand-Dyed Fabrics Made Easy*. Bothell, Wash.: That Patchwork Place, 1996.

Dietrich, Mimi, and Roxi Eppler. *The Easy Art of Appliqué*. Bothell, Wash.: That Patchwork Place, 1994.

Doak, Carol. *Quiltmaker's Guide: Basics & Beyond*. Paducah, Ky.: Schroeder Publishing, 1991.

Dunnewold, Jane. *Complex Cloth*. Bothell, Wash.: That Patchwork Place, 1996.

Gaber, Susan. *Treasury of Flower Designs*. Mineola, N. Y.: Dover Publications, 1981.

Hallock, Anita, & Betsy Hallock Heath. *Fast Patch Kids' Quilts*, Iola, Wis.: Chilton Book Co., 1996.

Haysom, Cari. *StampCraft* . Radnor, Pa.: Chilton Book Co., 1996.

Hoever, Judy, and Larry Quintman. *Quilt Labels Made Easy, vols. I & II*. North Branch, N. J.: Patches, Inc., 1996.

McKelvey, Susan. *Friendship's Offering*. Lafayette, Calif.: C&T Publishing, 1990.

———. *Scrolls & Banners to Trace*. Millersville, Md.: Wallflower Designs, 1990.

———. *More Scrolls & Banners to Trace*. Millersville, Md.: Wallflower Designs.

———. *The Signature Quilt*. Saddle Brook, N. J.: Quilt House Publishing, 1995.

———. *See-to-Trace Pad*. Millersville, Md.: Wallflower Designs.

———. *Traceables from the Baltimore Album Quilts at the Maryland Historical Society*. Millersville, Md.: Wallflower Designs.

———. *A Treasury of Quilt Labels*. Lafayette, Calif.: C&T Publishing,1992.

———. *Limitless Labels to Trace*. Millersville, Md.: Wallflower Designs, 1996.

Michell, Marti. *Quilting for People Who Don't Have Time to Quilt*. San Marcos, Calif.: American School of Needlework, Inc., 1988.

Munsch, Robert. *Love You Forever*. Willowdale, Ontario, Canada: Firefly Books Ltd., 1986/1996.

Nelson, Cyril, and Carter Houck. *Treasury of Antique Quilts*. Avenel, N. J.: Wings Books, 1995.

Seelig, Jane. *Fabric Inkin'*. Danville, Ill.: Grace Publications, 1996.

Simms, Ami. *Creating Scrapbook Quilts*. Flint, Mich.: Mallery Press, 1993.

Smith, Nancy J., and Lynda S. Milligan. *Penstitch and Lettering*. Denver, Colo.: Possibilities, 1996.

Walner, Hari. *Trapunto by Machine*. Lafayette, Calif: C&T Publishing, 1996.

Weiland, Barbara, ed. *All New! Copy Art for Quilters*. Bothell, Wash.: That Patchwork Place, 1995.

Resources

Suppliers: *These suppliers may carry additional items not listed here.*

American Quilter's Society
PO Box 3290
Paducah KY 42002-3290
Web: www.AQSquilt.com
E-mail: AQSquilt@apex.net
membership, book sales, annual quilt show, quarterly magazine

Batiks Etcetera
Jan Smiley, owner
411 Pine Street
Fort Mill SC 29715
Phone: (800) 228-4573
Web: www.batiks.com
E-mail: batiks@cetlink.net
mail order only; batik fabrics, fabric dyeing, and stamping supplies

Block Party Studios
922 L Avenue
Nevada IA 50201
Phone: (800) 419-2812
E-mail: blockparty@nevia.net
preprinted labels, Y&C pens

Brandywine Design
PO Box 135
Chanhassen MN 55317
Twelve Days of Christmas patterns and The Critters Quilt Book

Burkell, Marge
4638 Basswood
Erie PA 16506
Noshi pattern

Changing Seasons
Penguin USA
375 Hudson Street
New York NY 10024
book with fan pattern

Laura Chapman
743 Willow Lake Road
Charleston, SC 29412

Cherrywood Fabrics
361 Cherrywood Drive North
Baxter MN 56401
Phone: (218) 829-0967
hand-dyed fabrics

**Chosen Sisters
Heirloom Labels**
3507 264th Avenue SE
Issaquah WA 98029
Fax: 425-557-2408
E-mail: quilt4joy@aol.com
custom quilt labels

Churbuck, Kim
1140 East Columbia Avenue
Davenport IA 52803
Phone: (319) 324-8128
E-mail: KChurbuck@aol.com
label design books; Permawriter II, Micron Pigma .01 sets and brush sets in nine colors; muslin for label making; light boxes

Clotilde Inc.
PO Box 3000
Louisiana MO 63353-3000
Phone: (800) 772-2891
call for a free comprehensive catalog of notions for stitchers

Connecting Threads
PO Box 8940
Vancouver WA 98668-8940
Phone: (800) 574-6454
books, pens, Ott-Lite, light tables, stitchers' notions; call for a free catalog

**Covered Bridge
Quilt Supply**
PO Box 333
Winterset IA 50273
Phone: (515) 462-1020
photo-transfer paper

Design Plus
Heidi Hoff Wurst
Web: www.QuiltBroker.com
E-mail: lv2quilt@frii.com
quilt labels, care labels, pens

Dharma Trading Co.
PO Box 150916
San Rafael CA 94915
Phone: (800) 542-5227
fabric dyes and Retayne

D. J. Inkers
by Dianne J. Hook
Phone: (800) 325-4890
Web: www.djinkers.com
computer software

Dover Publications, Inc.
31 East Second Street
Mineola, NY 11501
Web: www.zedcor.com
*more than 800 books with all
types of copy art*

Electric Quilt Company
Phone: (800) 356-4219
Web:
www.wcnet.org/ElectricQuiltCo/
E-mail: equiltco@wcnet.org
*EQ3; QuilText, QuiltBlock, and
QuiltBlock Too software*

**Environmental Lighting
Concepts, Inc.**
3923 Coconut Palm Drive
Tampa FL 33619
Phone (for information only):
(800) 842-8848
Ott-Lite manufacturer

Fancywork
Kathy O'Hara Light
1718 Lakewood Avenue
Lima OH 45805
Phone: (419) 223-3506
preprinted labels

Friendly Impressions
PO Box 1333
Redondo Beach CA 90278
rubber stamps

Good Books
Intercourse PA 17534
"Country Songbird Quilt"
©1990

Grace, Gladys
213 Killingly Road
Pomfret Center CT 06259
Phone: (800) 650-4121 or
(860) 928-2034
*stenciling supplies; catalog is
$3.50*

Graphics 2000
1112 East 15th Street
Plano TX 75074
Phone: (972) 516-6618
photo-transfer service

Hancock's of Paducah
Phone: (800) 845-8723
Web:
www.Hancocks-Paducah.com
E-mail: hanpad@sunsix.infi.net
*fabric and notions; call for a free
catalog*

Hot Potatoes
Suite 311
209 10th Avenue South
Nashville TN 37203
Phone: (615) 255-4055
Fax: (615) 255-4556
stamping supplies

Imagination Station
7571 Crater Lake Hwy. #101
White City OR 97503
Phone: (800) 338-3857
photo-transfer service

JD Stencils
PO Box 3764
Cerritos CA 90703-3764
Phone: (562) 860-1128
*stencils, Pigma pens, and light
tables; catalog is $1.00*

Keepsake Quilting
PO Box 1618
Centre Harbor NH 03226-1618
Phone: (800) 865-9458
Web: www.keepsakequilting.com
E-mail: keepsake@lr.net
*Pigma pens, light tables, Ott-Lite,
labels, label stamps, label book-
lets, EQ3 software, stationery,
books, photo-transfer paper, other
quilters' notions; call for a free
catalog*

Little Foot, Ltd.
605 Bledsoe NW
Albuquerque NM 87107
Phone: (505) 345-7647
Ott-Lite and acrylic tables

Mallery Press
4206 Sheraton Drive
Flint MI 48532-3557
Phone: (800) A-STITCH
(278-4824)
Web: http://quilt.com/amisimms
*books by Ami Simms and Photos
to Fabric transfer paper; Ami's
book, Creating Scrapbook Quilts
lists several companies that do
photo transfers and gives com-
parative information about each
of them.*

Martingale & Company
PO Box 118
Bothell WA 98041-0118
Phone: (800) 426-3126
Fax: (425) 486-7596
Web: www.patchwork.com
E-mail: info@patchwork.com
fiber and quilting books and tools

Me Sew Co.
Suite 195
24307 Magic Mountain Parkway
Valencia CA 91355
Phone: (800) 846-3739
light tables

Myoraku, Amy
9101 172nd Avenue NE
Redmond WA 98052
Myomi pattern

Nancy's Notions
Phone: (800) 833-0690
Web: www.nancysnotions.com
*free comprehensive catalog
of notions for stitchers*

Papercuttings by Alison
PO Box 2771
Sarasota FL 34230
Phone: (941) 957-0328
or (941) 952-0763
silhouette designs

Patches
Judy Hoever, owner
6226 Ingleside Drive
Wilmington, NC 28409
Phone: (910) 792-9198
E-mail: LAQ1@aol.com
label designs to trace

Pelle's
PO Box 242
Davenport CA 95017
*Pelle's See-Thru Stamps and
stamping supplies*

Personal Stamp Exchange
#324
345 South McDowell Boulevard
Petaluma CA 94954
Phone: (707) 588-8058
rubber stamps

**Picture Perfect
Photo Quilts**
8622 Ault Lane
Morrison CO 80465
Phone: (303) 697-1396
E-mail: mspears@rmii.com
photo-transfer service

Pro Chemical & Dye, Inc.
Phone: (800) 2-BUY-DYE
fabric dyes and Retayne

QuiltClips
Carolyn Kissell
PO Box 99204
Raleigh NC 27624-9204
E-mail: QuiltClips@aol.com
computer clip art

Quiltmakers
9658 Plano Road
Dallas TX 75238
quiltmakers' photo-transfer paper

Quilts & Other Comforts
1 Quilter's Lane
Box 4100
Golden CO 80402-4100
Phone: (800) 881-6624
Web:
www.quiltsandothercomforts.com
*Ott-Lite, EQ3, Speedball Fabric
Painters, books, and quilters'
supplies; call for a free catalog*

Rubber Stampede
PO Box 246
Berkeley CA 94708
Phone: (510) 420-6800
rubber stamps and accessories

Seattle Woodworks, Ltd.
13032 Robinhood Lane
Snohomish WA 98290
Phone: (800) 357-9663
light tables

Skills Graphics
Anita Tinlin
5225 Willow Mill Drive
Marietta GA 30068
Phone: (770) 565-0889
Fax: (770) 972-7970
E-mail:
anitat @atl.mindspring.com
Quilt Image stationery

SPPS, Inc.
Quiltime
#165
4410 North Rancho Drive
Las Vegas NV 89130
Phone: (800) 982-8525 (orders) or
(702) 658-7133
E-mail: sppcinc@ix.netcom.com
  or sppcince@aol.com
Web: www.quiltime.com
*QuilText, QuiltBlock, QuiltBlock
Too, and ClipArt for Quilters*

**Sweet Memories Publishing
Co.**
2701 Hillsdale Court
Green Bay WI 54313
wildflower designs

Stamps Happen, Inc.
369 South Acacia Avenue
Fullerton CA 92831
rubber stamps

Thread Pro
E-mail: thredpro@airmail.net
Stitch & Ditch fabric stabilizer

Wallflower Design
Susan McKelvey
1161 Goldfinch Lane
Millersville MD 21108
*books, pens, and other
quilt-signing products*

ZimPrints
Phone: (423) 584-9430
stamping supplies

Web Sites and E-mail Addresses

Just a few of the hundreds of places to go on the web and net!

Amazon.com
Web: www.Amazon.com
"Earth's biggest bookstore"

American Quilt Study Group
Web: http://catsis.weber.edu/aqsg
E-mail: aqsg@juno.com
a network of quilt lovers interested in quilt history; membership, quarterly newsletter, research library

Dover Publication's Clip-Art and Pictorial Archives
Web: www.zedcor.com

Links We Love
Web: www.craftsearch.com/Quilt/links.html
has links to 1000+ quilt-related Web sites

National Quilters Association, Inc.
Web: www.his.com/~queenb/nqa
E-mail: nqa@erds.com
membership, teachers, appraisals, annual quilt show, quarterly magazine, National Quilting Day

Planet Patchwork
Web: www.tvq.com/index.html *or* www.planetpatchwork.com/index.html
"Where the world's quilters come for information and inspiration."

Web: www.tvq.com/qltprogs.htm
unbiased, in-depth examination of various software for quilt design

Web: www.tvq.com/links.htm
links to and reviews of many useful, informative, and entertaining sites

Patchwords
Web: www.patchwords.com/
a frequently updated Internet community; watch for updated information about printing on fabric using computers.

Quilter's Newsletter Magazine
E-mail: qnm@quiltersnewsletter.com
Web: www.quiltersnewsletter.com

Stamp.Net Gazette
Web: www.delphi.com/crafts/gazette.html
"All the Stamping Stuff We Can POSSIBLY Fit"

Tidbits and Trinkets
Web: www.az.com/~karenm/tnt.html
quotes for quilters

World Wide Quilting Page
Web: http://quilt.com/MainQuiltingPage.html
"The mother of all quilting sites!"; has links to many other Web sites

Web: http://ttsw.com/quiltstorespage.html
quilt-store listings

Web: http://ttsw.com/quiltshowspage.html
quilt-show listings

About the Author

Margo J. Clabo wandered into the wonderful world of quiltmaking in 1991, where she found that beautiful quilts could be created with a sewing machine. Since then, she has been involved with quilters at both the local and statewide level, has taught machine-quilting techniques, and has entered her quilts in regional and national shows. Because she felt it was important to add labels to her own quilts, Margo began taking photographs of special labels found on quilts at the shows she attended and collecting information about different techniques that could be used to make unique labels. This book is the result of that research.

Margo and her husband, Alvin, live in Cleveland, Tennessee, and have two grown sons.

Publications and Products

Many titles are available at your local quilt shop.
For more information, write for a free color catalog
to Martingale & Company, PO Box 118, Bothell,
WA 98041-0118 USA.

☎ U.S. and Canada, call **1-800-426-3126** for the
name and location of the quilt shop nearest you.
Int'l: 1-425-483-3313   Fax: 1-425-486-7596
E-mail: info@patchwork.com
Web: www.patchwork.com   2.98